A Song for Seven Mountains

52 weeks of inspirational thoughts and song starters

ISBN-13: 978-1534724983
ISBN-10: 1534724982

**S🌐UNDS of
the NATIONS**

6391 Leisure Town Road
Vacaville, CA 95687
dano@missionvacaville.org

Table of Contents

What you will get from this journal?

Songwriting Experience

Songwriters write songs. I know it sounds simple, but the truth is that many people who can write songs just don't. By giving you a specific assignment each week, you will grow stronger at songwriting just by doing what you already love to do—writing songs. I guarantee that if you write a song every week for a year and follow the songwriting tips in each lesson, *you will end up a stronger songwriter at the end of the year.*

Knowledge of Song Craft

This journal will also strengthen your understanding of song craft. In each lesson there is a devotional thought, an assignment, a songwriting tip, and a place for you to write down your song ideas. The songwriting tips come from my more than thirty years of songwriting experience featuring

1

material from my books, classes, and training events. In my travels around the world, I have literally empowered tens of thousands of people to write their first or best song. By paying attention to these tips and applying them to your songwriting, *you will be moving from self-expression to true communication through utilizing the art of song craft.*

What Are the Seven Mountains?

In 1975, three world changers from three different continents and denominations had a similar revelation. That revelation was that if believers are to impact any nation for Jesus Christ, we must affect more than the church; we must love and serve every mountain of society. Bill Bright, founder of Campus Crusade, Loren Cunningham, founder of Youth With a Mission, and Francis Schaeffer, founder of L'Abri community in Switzerland defined the seven mountains or pillars of society as business, government, media, arts and entertainment, education, family, and religion.

This mandate reminds me of a quote from the seventeenth century French economist, philosopher, and mathematician, Blaise Pascal. Pascal said, "It's not those who write the laws who have the greatest impact on society. It's those who write the songs." Songs are powerful tools for influencing the culture of any generation. I believe songs possess the power to educate children, shape governments, restore marriages and families, promote healing, advance ideas, prosper businesses, comfort and sooth the heart, inform the mind, and inspire the soul. *A Song for Seven Mountains* seeks to train songwriters to impact all of society with the love and grace of Jesus Christ through the powerful medium of music.

A Discovery of Your Primary Sphere of Influence

Knowing who your audience is empowers you to write better songs. Experimenting each week with one of the seven mountains will lead you to be able to define the area of your primary grace and calling by the end of the year. Once you know your target audience, *you can begin to focus your writing efforts around a specific audience which will then improve the strength of your writing voice.*

Basically, I guarantee three results if you truly follow through with this one-year devotional journal. You *will increase* your songwriting experience, you *will improve* your skill and knowledge of song craft, and you *will strengthen* your writing voice by discovering your primary sphere of influence. That is a one-year commitment worth making!

A Brief Introduction to Songwriting

Start with a Song Hook

Most great commercial songwriters identify their song hook before attempting to compose a song. The song hook tells what your song is all about in as few words and musical notes as possible. The average song hook is one to five words long, and it is often the title of the song. As its name suggests, a song hook should catch your listeners' attention, keep their interest, and take them somewhere. Composing from a song hook is the method you will use in this journal.

The Purpose of Song Sections

After you have crafted a song hook, you are ready to build song sections. Song sections are the building blocks for song writing. Though there are many types and variations of song sections, there are three major song sections that are the main building blocks of most songs.

Verse – conveys context, content, and any vital information about your song.

Chorus – features the song hook.

Bridge – refreshes interest in the hook through musical, lyrical, and rhythmic contrast.

The Basic Song Forms

Putting these song sections together creates a song. The order and fashion in which you put the song sections together creates a song form. There are several basic song forms that most crafted songs will fit into.

Verse/Chorus – This is the most common and popular form of our day. In this form, the verse usually comes first, and the chorus follows, emphasizing the hook through melodic or lyrical repetition. Verse/chorus song form may also use a bridge section to refresh the hook idea or a pre-chorus section to lyrically and melodically build into the hook.

AABA or Chorus/Bridge – This is the strongest song form for a song hook that doesn't require a set-up of context or information. In this song form, the song hook is the first line of the song. The second song section is called a bridge. It builds or lifts musically but does not contain the melody or lyrics of the song hook.

AAA or Chorus Only – This is the best song form for compositions with storylines or a lot of information because it features a single song section. The song hook appears as the first or last line of the song and is usually not repeated again in the song unless there are multiple versions of the one song section. AAA song form is the template most used for composing classic and modern hymns.

Tools for Building Song Sections

The three most common tools for building song sections are repetition, lists, and contrasting ideas. Let's examine each of these briefly.

Repetition – When you have a great idea or a strong line, why not just repeat it? Song craft utilizes several forms of repetition for crafting chorus sections:

- **Every Line Repetition** repeats the song hook four times.
- **Triple Repetition** repeats the song hook through three lines followed by one summation line.
- **Double or Paired Repetition** repeats the song hook twice followed by two contrasting lines.
- **Alternating Repetition** repeats the song hook every other line with contrasting lines in between.
- **First and Last Repetition** repeats the song hook in the first and last line of the song section with two complimentary lines in between.

Never be afraid to use these simple repetition tools to feature your hook in a chorus section.

Lists – These are often used for building verses, but they also appear in chorus and bridge sections of many worship songs.

- **The Key Word or Phrase List** uses a repeated phrase on each line. For example, if the key phrase was "She walked…," you might construct your verse with the following lines:

> She walked into my heart
> She walked into my head
> She walked into my world
> From the first words that she said

You can see that the key word or phrase list uses one repeated phrase where you essentially fill in the blank with your strongest thoughts and ideas.

- **A Unique List** features three to four original ideas in a list form:

> There is beauty in her smile
> Grace in her walk
> Strength in her soul
> She's so much more than talk

In this list form, all the ideas are connected, but no words or phrases are repeated. It is simply a unique list of complimentary ideas focused towards a single thought.

Contrasting or Opposite Ideas – These are used for any type of song section. They are probably most often used in a verse but can also form strong chorus or bridge sections. With this tool, you simply pit two contrasting or complimentary ideas against each other to build the song section:

> In my *weakness* you stood *strong*,
> When I *fell* you *carried* me,

In my *desperate* nights your *hope,*
Showed me who I want to be.

These three simple tools for building song sections can be identified in many of your favorite marketplace songs. Don't stumble over their simplicity. These tools are the trade secrets of successful songwriters that make a song more memorable and therefore more singable.

For more complete instructions on these introductory thoughts as well as more tips and tools on songwriting, see my songwriting books and resources listed in the back of this journal.

Now, that you have acquainted or refreshed yourself with the basics of songwriting, let's begin this exciting one-year journey together!

Week 1

The Mountain of Religion

Welcome to the first step of our one-year journey together. Let's start this year off by crafting an adoration song that could be used in a church for congregational worship on a Sunday morning. Adoration songs have been a foundational sub-genre for gospel writers like seven-time Grammy Award winner Kirk Franklin in his song "Jesus, You Are." Kirk's song answers the question that Jesus asked His disciples. That question stands as perhaps the most important query in the kingdom of God. Let's examine that text together.

Matthew 16:14 (NIV)

14 "But what about you?" he (Jesus) asked. "Who do you say that I am?"

Song Idea

This week's assignment is to write an adoration song for congregational worship that centers around your answer to the question, "Who is God to you?" Write a song about it. Before you start writing, remember to really focus on what the main idea of your song is. Every great song has one main idea. The best songs have one universal song theme that everyone in your target audience can relate to. Write out one to three sentences that express the main idea of your song.

Song Hook

The song hook contains the main idea of the song in as few words and musical notes as possible presented in one well-stated word or phrase. Write your song hook idea in one to five words in the space below.

Songwriting Tip

Hooks are used to catch. Make sure your song hook is lyrically and melodically catchy. It is the most important feature of your song. Take time to make it great.

Title:

Music and Lyrics by:

13

Title:

Music and Lyrics by:

Week 2

The Mountain of Family

In 1971, Neil Diamond was nominated for his first Grammy Award in the category of best pop vocal performance. The song titled "I Am… I Said" was a cry to discover his personal identity. Diamond went on to be inducted into the Songwriters Hall of Fame and the Rock and Roll Hall of Fame as the third most successful adult contemporary artist in Billboard chart history.

Personal identity is a huge subject in songwriting. We see a great example in the Bible. Right after Peter expressed his revelation of who Jesus Christ was to him, Jesus spoke to Peter's identity. I believe this points to the second most important question in the kingdom of God, "Who does Jesus say that you are?" A revelation of how Jesus saw Peter is the very next thing that Jesus shares with his disciple. Let's pick up the story on the next page.

Matthew 16:17-19 (NIV)

17 Jesus replied, "Blessed are you, Simon son of Jonah, for this was not revealed to you by flesh and blood, but by my Father in heaven. 18 And I tell you that you are Peter, and on this rock I will build my church, and the gates of Hades will not overcome it. 19 I will give you the keys of the kingdom of heaven; whatever you bind on earth will be bound in heaven, and whatever you loose on earth will be loosed in heaven."

Song Idea

Being a healthy member of a family starts with a healthy personal identity. This week's assignment is to write an identity song. Ask God who He says you are. Write down some of His answers to that question below to form song ideas.

Song Hook

Choose one of the ideas God spoke concerning your identity and craft it into a song hook of one to five words.

Songwriting Tip

Even when writing about something personal, your song content should still be such that everyone can relate to it, especially if you intend to publish your song. When writing something personal, make sure your subject still reflects a universal song theme.

Title:

Music and Lyrics by:

Title

Music and Lyrics by:

Week 3

The Mountain of Government

In the last two weeks, we crafted songs around the identity of God and around your personal identity. It is also possible to craft a song around the God-given identity of a nation. I met a young lady who composed a national identity song around what she heard God saying over a small island nation. One day, she had the opportunity to share that song with the president of the nation. The president was so moved by her musical inspiration that he declared that for as long as he was in office, her song would be performed alongside their national anthem every time it was sung. Patriotic songs can reveal a corporate identity representing what God is saying over a large group of people, a city, a region, or even a nation.

1 Peter 2:9 (NIV)

But you are a chosen people, a royal priesthood, a holy nation, God's special possession, that you may declare the praises of him who called you out of darkness into his wonderful light.

Song Idea

Patriotism can be defined as a love, loyalty, defense, or devotion for one's country. Your assignment this week is to craft a patriotic song based upon what God is saying over your nation. What is God speaking into the identity of your nation? What strength or virtue would He encourage? Write your thoughts below.

Song Hook

Craft a song hook of one to five words that forms the basis of a patriotic song in the space below.

Songwriting Tip

Since a patriotic song is crafted to be inspirational, your chorus section needs a definite high point. The melody and lyric of your chorus should build into this high point which is usually featured at the end of the chorus and expresses the key idea of the song with the highest note in the melodic range.

Title:

Music and Lyrics by:

Title:

Music and Lyrics by:

Week 4

The Mountain of Arts and Entertainment

Record companies are not the only entities looking for great songs. Have you ever thought about composing for an art gallery? In 1950, Ray Evans and Jay Livingston crafted a song inspired by the renaissance portrait of Leonardo da Vinci. That year, the song "Mona Lisa" won the Academy Award for best original song. In 1992, Nat King Cole's version of the song was inducted into the Grammy Hall of Fame. Cole described this song as one of his favorites among all his recordings. There are many noble topics and markets for the aspiring songwriter.

Psalm 45:1 (NIV)

My heart is stirred by a noble theme as I recite my verses for the king; my tongue is the pen of a skillful writer.

Song Idea

This week's assignment is to imagine that a famous art gallery has commissioned you to write a song based upon a specific piece of art in their upcoming exhibition. Search online for a specific piece of art that inspires you. Write some of your observations on the subject of your painting in the space below.

Song Hook

Now craft a song hook that relates directly to the title or subject of your chosen work of art in the space below.

Songwriting Tip

One of the primary rules of songwriting is, "Show me; don't tell me." This assignment is the perfect chance to show your skill at using imagery to inspire vision and emotion. Recreate the picture of this painting with your lyric craft and musical mood.

Title:

Music and Lyrics by:

29

Title:

Music and Lyrics by:

Week 5

The Mountain of Media

Television news channels have their own demand for original musical compositions in the form of a "news music package." News music packages consist of the following musical pieces: opens, closes, bumpers, topicals, franchise stingers, IDs, utility tracks, and billboards. Each of these themes are crafted into different formats and lengths usually with versions in 60-, 30-, 20-, 15-, and 10-second forms. Some stations opt to use popular songs for their news package — like KNTV in San Jose, California, which used Burt Bacharach and Hal Davis's Grammy Award winning hit "Do You Know the Way to San Jose" sung by Dionne Warwick. The main quality of a news music package is that it has a sound that catches your attention for a specific announcement. Using a certain sound, instrument, or musical motif to gather people's attention for an announcement is an ancient practice. You can read in Bible times how different blasts on the trumpet were used to communicate various announcements.

Hosea 5:8 (NIV)

8 Sound the trumpet in Gibeah, the horn in Ramah. Raise the battle cry in Beth Aven; lead on Benjamin.

Song Idea

This week's assignment is to imagine you have been asked by the local media to write a new 60-second topical intro for a sports program. The music should catch your attention and sound active. Only the first thirty seconds of your composition should contain lyrics. What lyrics would you craft for this pitch? Capture your best ideas in the space provided below.

Song Hook

Even a jingle or news theme has a dominant lyrical or musical hook. Craft your hook for this pitch in the space below.

Songwriting Tip

Since this song assignment is predominantly musical, this is a great time to mention musical motif. A motif is a short musical idea, a few musical notes, or a song fragment that repeats throughout the song to emphasize thematic identity. Repetition and proper use of this smallest structural musical unit makes a song more memorable.

Title:

Music and Lyrics by:

Title:

Music and Lyrics by:

Week 6

The Mountain of Education

Alma (Latin for "nourishing") mater (Latin for "mother") is an allegorical phrase meant to imply that a school provides intellectual nourishment to its students. An alma mater also refers to the anthem of a school, college, or university. The oldest school anthem belongs to Cornell University. It was written in 1872 by student roommates and set to the tune of "Annie Lisle," a popular ballad from 1857. The song is the official alma mater of at least 31 colleges and universities. Imagine the hundreds of thousands of people who have a sentimental connection to this song. One way to impact society with your music is to write an alma mater.

Proverbs 10:21 (NIV)

10 The lips of the righteous nourish many, but fools die for lack of sense.

Song Idea

Your assignment this week is to serve the mountain of education. Start by researching a local school. Find out if it has a school song (alma mater) or not. If it has one, then consider modernizing or updating it. If there is no school song or if a new one is needed, craft an original song for this local school or college. Write some virtues of this school below.

Song Hook

Craft a song hook that relates directly to the name of the school or a dominant characteristic of that school in the space provided below.

Songwriting Tip

In the introduction of this journal, we described the list method of forming song sections. Listing virtues of a particular school could form an easy verse section for this assignment.

Title:

Music and Lyrics by:

_____

_____

_____

_____

_____

_____

_____

_____

_____

_____

_____

_____

_____

_____

_____

_____

_____

_____

Copyright is Today's Date:

39

Title:

Music and Lyrics by:

Week 7

The Mountain of Business

Not every hit song or musical money maker comes in a standard song form. Some of the most memorable song bits come from jingles embedded in product advertisements. Jingles are a great opportunity to learn the wisdom of a different type of song craft. According to a 2011-2012 Film and Television Music Salary and Rate Survey, jingle writers in that time period sold their work for an average of $10,000 per jingle to local or regional markets. That's not a bad day's work. God said to Daniel that when he set his mind to gain understanding, his words were heard.

Daniel 10:12 (NIV)

12 Then he continued, "Do not be afraid, Daniel. Since the first day that you set your mind to gain understanding and to humble yourself before your God, your words were heard..."

Song Idea

In this week's assignment, imagine that a national burger chain has asked you to compose their next jingle for a television and online campaign. Remember that a jingle is often only 30 to 60 seconds in length and uses repetition. You may want to research some past jingles from this brand to get an idea of what type of lyric this company is drawn to. Write some ideas below that you think would help feature the strengths of this product.

Song Hook

Now craft your memorable song hook in the space below.

Songwriting Tip

Memorability is hugely important in songwriting but even more so in a jingle. Give your songs the memorability test. Play the song for a person; he or she should be able to hum or whistle the dominant melody of the song after hearing it only one time.

Title:

Music and Lyrics by:

_____

_____

_____

_____

_____

_____

_____

_____

_____

_____

_____

_____

_____

_____

_____

_____

_____

_____

_____

_____

_____

_____

Copyright is Today's Date:

43

Title:

Music and Lyrics by:

Week 8

The Mountain of Religion

Two months ago, you crafted an adoration song based on who Jesus is to you. This week you will craft another type of corporate worship song: a sung petition. Many cultures and religions sing their prayers. Prayer songs can also become popular in the market place. "The Prayer," a duet sung by Celine Dion and Andrea Bocelli, was nominated for a Golden Globe Award, Academy Award, and Grammy Award. Prayer songs are a powerful way of connecting with God and releasing our most earnest longings. In the following psalm, David shares his deepest prayer desire with God.

Psalm 27:4 (NIV)

One thing I ask from the LORD, this only do I seek: that I may dwell in the house of the LORD all the days of my life, to gaze on the beauty of the LORD and to seek him in his temple.

Song Idea

We know that we can ask God anything, anytime. But imagine for a moment that you had one request that you know for certain would not be denied. What would you ask God for? What is your "one thing I ask..."? This week's assignment is to craft a petition song surrounding your deepest desire. Brainstorm your desires as song ideas in the space below.

Song Hook

In a petition worship song, the hook is always in the form of a question. Write your petition below in the form of a question.

Songwriting Tip

Repetition is the most common and fundamental way to feature a song hook. Don't be afraid to use repetition because it is simple. After all, if you write a great line, why not repeat it?

Title:

Music and Lyrics by:

Title:

Music and Lyrics by:

Week 9

The Mountain of Family

In 1984, the British-American rock band Foreigner released the power ballad "I Want to Know What Love Is." The song reached double-platinum and was nominated for Grammy Awards for song of the year and best pop performance. People are hungry to know and understand true love. The seventeenth century French philosopher and mathematician Blaise Pascal said, "It is not those who write the laws that have the greatest impact on society but those who write the songs."

Love and marriage are topics that have been radically redefined in the last few years. The new definitions often do not match biblical values. I wonder if this confusion is because Christians have not been writing love songs. If our songs are truly more powerful then our laws, then I think followers of Jesus can redefine marriage by writing the greatest love songs on earth. After all, the longest song in the Bible is a love song.

Song of Songs 1:1-2 (NIV)

1 Solomon's Song of Songs. 2 She: Let him kiss me with the kisses of his mouth—for your love is more delightful than wine.

Song Idea

Your assignment this week is to craft a love song that rekindles romance in marriage. Capture the ideas of romance and marriage in your song without actually using the words "romance" and "marriage." Write down synonyms and word pictures for these two concepts in the space provided below.

Song Hook

Craft a song hook that will be the feature of your romantic song in the space below.

Songwriting Tip

Avoid using typical clichés like "love is blind" or "love is in the air." Be original.

Title:

Music and Lyrics by:

Title:

Title:

Music and Lyrics by:

Week 10

The Mountain of Government

In 1938, with the rise of Adolf Hitler, a Jewish-Russian immigrant named Irving Berlin released the song "God Bless America" on Armistice Day. Sixty-three years later, Canadian pop star Celine Dion performed the song on national TV following the September 11, 2001, terrorist attacks. Sony Music Entertainment released a benefit album called *God Bless America* which featured Dion singing the song. The album hit number one on the Billboard charts showing that a well-crafted prayer for a nation can have wide public appeal.

2 Chronicles 7:14 (NIV)

14 "If my people, who are called by my name, will humble themselves and pray and seek my face and turn from their wicked ways, then I will hear from heaven, and I will forgive their sin and will heal their land."

Song Idea

Two weeks ago, you crafted a prayer song around your greatest personal desire. This week, your assignment is to craft a prayer over your city, region, or nation. You are composing for the mountain of government not the church, so make sure your lyrics have a cross-platform public appeal. Write your ideas below.

Song Hook

Remember that the song hook on a petition song appears in the form of a question. What are you asking on behalf of your nation?

Songwriting Tip

Customize don't compromise. You can use language that reflects a religious perspective without sounding religious by customizing your word selection. Avoid religious jargon or words that are only used or understood in church.

Title:

Music and Lyrics by:

_____

_____

_____

_____

_____

_____

_____

_____

_____

_____

_____

_____

_____

_____

_____

_____

_____

_____

_____

_____

_____

Music and Lyrics by:

Week 11

The Mountain of Arts and Entertainment

In 2015, country music surpassed pop and rock, earning the number one position in hearts of Americans by capturing 17 percent of the national interest. Country music as a genre has uniquely been able to speak to the topics of faith and values without sounding religious. Consider the song "Jesus Take the Wheel" written by Brett James, Hillary Lindsey and Gordie Sampson and recorded by country music artist Carrie Underwood. The song tells the story of a woman crying out to Jesus to take control of her life during an emergency, yet it took the 2005 Grammy Award for best country song and also won single of the year at the 2005 Academy of Country Music Awards.

This week's assignment is to craft a song to pitch to a country music artist who is popular today. Choose your country artist, then craft your song on the subject of "home."

Psalm 127:1 (NIV)

Unless the LORD builds the house, the builders labor in vain. Unless the LORD watches over the city, the guards stand watch in vain.

Song Idea

Practice writing to give voice to someone beyond yourself. This will make you a stronger songwriter. How would your chosen artist view the concept of home? Capture your ideas below.

Song Hook

Your song hook below should be a short compelling declaration of the value of home.

Songwriting Tip

Prosody is the marriage between melody and prose. In simple terms, it means that your song should sound like what it says. When a song possesses great prosody, you can hear the music without the lyrics and still capture the essence of what it is saying. What melody creates a pleasing sense of home?

Title:

Music and Lyrics by:

Title:

Music and Lyrics by:

Week 12

The Mountain of Media

The music business landscape has drastically changed. Internet platforms like Spotify® and iTunes® have made it more challenging for the average musician to make money with music in the traditional ways. However, with the advent of thousands of television channels and millions of online broadcasts, music sync licensing is rising as the fastest route to music monetization for composers. This category of production music (also known as stock music or library music) refers to music that can be licensed to customers for use in film, television, radio, and other media. Wisdom for success in the music business is available to those who seek.

Proverbs 8:12 (KJV)

12 I wisdom dwell with prudence, and find out knowledge of witty inventions.

Song Idea

Practice your skill at creating production music for media. In this week's assignment, imagine that a film producer is doing a documentary on a nature park in your area. The producer is looking for a local artist to create a musical and lyrical backdrop that captures the physical essence of this park's beauty. Choose a park near you as your creative target. Write below some of the singable virtues of this location.

Song Hook

Craft your lyrical or melodic song hook about the nature park in the space provided below.

Songwriting Tip

Even instrumentals utilize the concept of a song hook. A song hook should be identifiable even without the accompanying lyric. To make sure your hook is really shining through, perform your composition for a friend without the lyric to see if they can identify the hook.

Title:

Music and Lyrics by:

_____
_____
_____
_____
_____
_____
_____
_____
_____
_____
_____
_____
_____
_____
_____
_____
_____
_____
_____
_____
_____
_____
_____
_____

Copyright is Today's Date:

Title:

Music and Lyrics by:

Week 13

The Mountain of Education

Sesame Street is a long-running children's television series that first aired in America in 1969. The program uses educational songs, animation, humor, and Jim Henson's Muppets to communicate educational content. A 1996 survey found that 95 percent of all American preschoolers had watched the show by the time they were three years old. As of 2014, *Sesame Street* had won 159 Emmy Awards and eight Grammy Awards. Educational music can be a valid and profitable pursuit for songwriting. The following Bible verse shows that King David used songs to teach his children.

Psalm 34:11 (NIV)

11 "Come, my children, listen to me: I will teach you the fear of the LORD." (Note that this is a psalm or song.)

Song Idea

For this week's assignment, practice creating an educational song focused on the parts of a plant. You can be as simple or as detailed as you would like. Write down the parts of a plant that you will focus on in your educational song in the space below.

Song Hook

Craft your simple, memorable song hook here. Have fun with this one.

Songwriting Tip

Creativity doesn't end with creating song. Your creativity needs to extend into the marketing of the song. Consider submitting your song to an educational website or making a music video. If *Sesame Street* won eight Grammy Awards, then there might be something significant in this for you also.

Title:

Music and Lyrics by:

_____

_____

_____

_____

_____

_____

_____

_____

_____

_____

_____

_____

_____

_____

_____

_____

_____

_____

_____

_____

_____

_____

Title:

Music and Lyrics by:

Week 14

The Mountain of Business

In 1982, George Thorogood and the Destroyers released the song "Bad to the Bone" on the album of the same name amidst moderate reviews. Though the fans initially didn't respond to the song, the mountains of entertainment and business swallowed it up. Television shows and movies started using it for the introductions of a "bad" character. Sporting events and commercials also picked up the song. Buick® ran a modified version of the song to advertise its Grand National vehicle for three years. What first appeared to be a flop on one mountain proved to be a huge commercial success in another. There is a time and place for every great song.

Ecclesiastes 3:1 (NIV)

1 There is a time for everything, and a season for every activity under the heavens;

Song Idea

Imagine that the Lexus® car brand has asked you to compose a song for the roll out of their new model. They used the words "stylish, elegant, classic, but not boring" to describe their pitch. Your assignment this week is to craft a song that could be featured as the backdrop for their commercial. Craft some lines below that reflect the image your clients are looking for.

Song Hook

Great songs always focus around one great idea. Write your central theme in a song hook of one to five words in the space below.

Songwriting Tip

Great imagery paints an idea without stating it. In this exercise, create a mood that is stylish, elegant, and classic without necessarily using those words. Use ideas and images that create the mood without directly stating the target.

Title:

Music and Lyrics by:

Title:

Music and Lyrics by:

Week 15

The Mountain of Religion

"Bless the Lord/10,000 Reasons" took the Song of the Year prize in the 2013 Gospel Music Awards. Even the title of this song strongly reflects how to craft an invocation song. An invocation song form possesses two parts. The first song part is an invitation usually calling the listener to a specific act of praise and worship. The second song part gives the reasons, revelations, or motivations for responding to God in this way. "10,000 Reasons" is a fresh way of expressing one of my favorite Bible verses.

Psalm 145:1 (AMPC)

Every day [with its new reasons] will I bless You [affectionately and gratefully praise You]; yes, I will praise Your name forever and ever.

Song Idea

Your assignment this week is to craft an invitational song that could be used for congregational worship. Choose a biblical expression of praise that you feel is missing in your church. Write below a list of reasons, revelations, and motivations that would inspire that specific response in a person.

Song Hook

Craft the song hook around your invitation. In one to five words invite someone to this specific act of worship.

Songwriting Tip

A song is not a sermon with three to five points. A song has one central theme clearly stated in a song hook. All other ideas in the song must point directly toward your song hook. Don't let your song become a tangle of competing ideas. Focus every thought at the target of your one best idea.

Title:

Music and Lyrics by:

_____

_____

_____

_____

_____

_____

_____

_____

_____

_____

_____

_____

_____

_____

_____

_____

_____

_____

_____

Copyright is Today's Date:

Title:

Music and Lyrics by:

Week 16

The Mountain of Family

This week's songwriting challenge is to compose a children's song. The children's category may be the most over-looked market for career songwriters. In the turbulent 1960's, a Bulgarian musician sought political asylum in the United States. After a radical encounter with God's love, Georgian Banov began to co-write and co-produce inspirational children's music. The *Music Machine* series and *Bullfrogs and Butterflies* sold over 3.5 million copies worldwide and earned Georgian both a Dove Award and a Grammy nomination.

Luke 18:16 (NIV)

16 But Jesus called the children to him and said, "Let the little children come to me, and do not hinder them, for the kingdom of God belongs to such as these."

Song Idea

When I wrote my first children's song I was shocked at how liberating it was. There is so much pressure to be cool, classy, and fresh when writing for an adult market. In a song for children, you can do every cheesy thing you ever wanted to do with a song. I found it incredibly refreshing. So here is your chance. What statements do you want to share with children? Write your thoughts below.

Song Hook

Now take your best idea and craft it into a song hook of one to five simply stated words.

Songwriting Tip

Simplicity is a key to strong songwriting in any musical genre. Certainly it is even more important when writing for children. Practice the strength of crafting powerful and potent lines that are simply expressed in words anyone could understand.

Title:

Music and Lyrics by:

_____

_____

_____

_____

_____

_____

_____

_____

_____

_____

_____

_____

_____

_____

_____

_____

_____

Copyright is Today's Date:

Title:

Music and Lyrics by:

Week 17

The Mountain of Government

Well-crafted songs on social issues often find their way into the mainstream market. In 1987, the "King of Pop" Michael Jackson released his classic record *Bad*. One of the singles from the hit album included "Man in the Mirror." The song stands as an uplifting and critically acclaimed pop ballad about society's tendency to turn away from difficult social issues. Michael's song and video acted as a literal call for change, challenging us with the message that transforming society starts by looking within.

Isaiah 58:6-8 (NIV)

6 Is not this the kind of fasting I have chosen: to loose the chains of injustice and untie the cords of the yoke, to set the oppressed free and break every yoke? **7** Is it not to share your food with the hungry and to provide the poor wanderer with shelter—when you see the naked, to clothe them, and not to turn away from your own flesh and blood? **8** Then your light will break forth like the dawn, and your healing will quickly appear; then your righteousness will go before you, and the glory of the LORD will be your read guard."

Song Idea

Writing for social justice without sounding preachy is a real challenge for believers. This week's assignment is to craft a marketplace song that speaks to a social issue needing reform. What subjects of social and cultural reform are you passionate about? Write your ideas below.

Song Hook

Capture your best song idea on social or cultural reform in a well-crafted song hook of one to five words.

Songwriting Tip

Musical and lyrical contrast is an important feature of any strong song. The theme of social justice is a great target for using contrasting lyrical ideas to build a song section.

Title:

Music and Lyrics by:

Title:

Music and Lyrics by:

Week 18

The Mountain of Entertainment

Max Martin started his career struggling as lead-singer for a long-haired glam rock band called Alive. Martin's secret was a hidden love of pop music. Today, he is considered a genius at crafting melodies. By 2014, Martin had written 21 number one singles in the US including songs for Britney Spears ("Baby One More Time"), NSync ("It's Gonna Be Me"), Pink ("So What"), Maroon 5 ("One More Night") and Katy Perry ("California Gurls" and "Teenage Dream"). Martin and his collaborators exerted such a strong influence on modern pop music that in 2014, his company supplied one quarter of all hits on the Billboard Hot 100 chart. Songwriters can be the people who put words in the mouths of others.

Exodus 4:15 (NIV)

15 You shall speak to him and put words in his mouth; I will help both of you speak and will teach you what to do.

Song Idea

Your assignment this week is to craft a song that you can pitch to someone already successful in the music business. Go to iTunes or Billboard and pick a pop artist from the top ten charts. Study that artist's top songs. What do they excel at? What are the strengths that make this artist successful— catchy choruses, memorable melodies, inspiring verses? Write their strengths in the space below.

Song Hook

Now craft a song hook that you could pitch to this artist for an upcoming music project.

Songwriting Tip

Memorable melodies utilize melodic motif, melodic emphasis, dramatic pauses, and magical moments. Research any of these terms you are not familiar with as they apply to song craft.

Title:

Music and Lyrics by:

Title:

Music and Lyrics by:

Week 19

The Mountain of Media

Russ Landau and David Vanacore's soundtrack to the reality television show *Survivor* hit the number nine spot in top internet albums of 2000. Their style showcased sounds of the south seas and dark rhythms from African jungles. This week it's your turn. A travel channel is looking for a production piece as the backdrop for an upcoming series on world travel.

Isaiah 42:10-11 (NIV)

10 Sing to the LORD a new song, his praise from the ends of the earth, you who go down to the sea, and all that is in, you islands, and all who live in them. 11 Let the wilderness and its towns raise their voices; let the settlements where Kedar

lives rejoice. Let the people of Sela sing for joy; let them shout from the mountaintops.

Song Idea

Your assignment this week is to craft a production piece for this travel series. Let the Bible passage be your inspiration for this assignment. Craft song ideas that capture the feel of each of the the locations mentioned in Isaiah 42:10-11.

Song Hook

Whether your composition this week has lyrics or not, it still should have an identifiable song hook and utilize tools like repetition. Capture your song hook for this assignment in the space below.

Songwriting Tip

When composing world/ethnic music, I like to start with an ethnic rhythm or melodic sample loop. These sound loops create an instant world feel that helps the song advance.

Title:

Music and Lyrics by:

_____
_____
_____
_____
_____
_____
_____
_____
_____
_____
_____
_____
_____
_____
_____
_____
_____
_____

Copyright is Today's Date:

Title:

Music and Lyrics by:

Week 20

The Mountain of Education

The most popular education song in the United States has to be the alphabet song copyrighted in 1835 by Charles Bradlee (officially titled "The A.B.C."). The melody comes from a Mozart piece called "Twelve Variations on Ah, vous dirai-je, maman" which Mozart borrowed from a French tune called, "Ah, vous dirai-je, maman" (Ah, Would I Tell You, Mother?) The same melody appears in "Twinkle, Twinkle, Little Star," "Baa, Baa, Black Sheep" as well as German and Hungarian Christmas carols. Imagine crafting a melody that is so memorable it endures two hundred years and crosses geographic and cultural boundaries.

1 Corinthians 14:7 (NIV)

7 Even in the case of lifeless things that make sounds, such as the pipe or harp, how will anyone know what tune is being

played unless there is a distinction in the notes?

Song Idea

Pursue distinct notes and a memorable melody in your assignment this week which is to craft an educational song teaching the parts of a sentence.

Song Hook

An educational song is a great place to utilize simple rhymes within the song hook. Craft your song hook in the space below.

Songwriting Tip

One form of rhyme abuse happens when writers rhyme too many lines. Generally, unless you are composing a rap song, alternate rhyming lines with non-rhyming ones.

Title:

Music and Lyrics by:

_____

_____

_____

_____

_____

_____

_____

_____

_____

_____

_____

_____

_____

_____

_____

_____

_____

_____

_____

_____

_____

Copyright is Today's Date:

Title:

Music and Lyrics by:

Week 21

The Mountain of Business

Radio and Records and *Billboard* magazines rank Barry Manilow as the top adult contemporary chart artist of all times, having sold over 75 million records worldwide. In 1978, five of his albums were on the best-seller charts simultaneously. Though Manilow is known for his hit musical recordings including "Mandy," "Weekend in New England," and "Copacabana," he is also among the most famous producers of all times of advertising jingles. Manilow has won CLIO awards for best television/cinema commercial for his composition of the jingle "Stuck on Me" for Johnson & Johnson® BAND-AID® brand, as well as an award for best international radio commercial for his performance in the jingle "Countdown" for Coca-Cola® company. He has also composed jingles for State Farm® Insurance and Stridex® medicated pads, demonstrating with his life that a great commercial pop songwriter and performer can also write great TV commercials.

Ecclesiastes 7:18 (NIV)

18 It is good to grasp the one and not let go of the other, the wise man will come away with them both.

Song Idea

Your business assignment this week is to put a new sound to an old jingle. Choose a famous old jingle for a product you love and update it. Write the lyrics from the old jingle in the space below.

Song Hook

Will you keep the same song hook, change it, or update it? Capture your idea in the space below.

Songwriting Tip

When all your songs begin to sound the same, try changing time signature (e.g. from 4/4 to 6/8), altering your song form (e.g. from verse/chorus to chorus/bridge AABA), or writing on a different instrument.

Title:

Music and Lyrics by:

Title:

Music and Lyrics by:

Week 22

The Mountain of Religion

"By My Side" was a declaration of biblical truth performed by Tenth Avenue North reminding us that God will never leave us or forsake us. This song composed by Mike Donehey, Phillip LaRue, and Jason Ingram received the Song of the Year award at the 2015 Dove Awards. Songs that declare truth are important because experience will often rise to the level of declaration.

John 14:6 (NIV)

8 Jesus answered, "I am the way and the truth and the life. No one comes to the Father except through me."

Song Idea

Declaration songs release biblical truths in a fresh, inspiring way. Your assignment this week is to craft the Bible verse on the previous page into a Scriptural declaration song that says the same thing using different words. Experiment with your main rewrite ideas and adapted lyrics in the space below.

Song Hook

Take your best idea from above and craft it into a song hook in the space below.

Songwriting Tip

Great song lyrics have balanced symmetry. Symmetry speaks of a pleasing proportion of parts, a similar or exact correspondence between different things. One way to achieve symmetry in your song lyrics is to match the syllable counts between alternating lines. In poetry, symmetry can also be referred to as the lyrical meter. Look for a pleasant balance in how your lyrics are constructed.

Title:

Music and Lyrics by:

_____

_____

_____

_____

_____

_____

_____

_____

_____

_____

_____

_____

_____

_____

_____

_____

_____

_____

_____

_____

_____

_____

_____

_____

Copyright is Today's Date:

Title:

Music and Lyrics by:

Week 23

The Mountain of Family

A lullaby or cradle-song is a simple and repetitive piece of music played for children or adults. Lullabies serve many purposes like assisting communication skills and regulating behavior, emotions, and attention. They are also often used as a sleep aid. Perhaps the most famous lullaby is "Wiegenlied" ("Good Evening, Good Night") composed by Johannes Brahms in 1868. The lullaby was dedicated to Brahms' friend on the occasion of the birth of her second son. It is widely rumored that Brahms' struggle with sleep apnea further motivated the composition of this piece.

Proverbs 3:24 (NIV)

24 When you lie down, you will not be afraid; when you lie down, your sleep will be sweet.

Song Idea

Your assignment this week is to compose a lullaby for the mountain of family. Your song should have a soothing melody and tempo with simple repetitive lyrics. Capture your song ideas in the space below.

Song Hook

Song hooks for lullabies often convey love, tenderness, and affection. Craft your song hook in the space below.

Songwriting Tip

Composing melodies a cappella (without instrumental accompaniment) helps your dominant melody line to not be restricted to your knowledge of chord structure. This is a favorite composition method of award winning writer Sting and worship writer Matt Redman.

Title:

Music and Lyrics by:

113

Title:

Music and Lyrics by:

Week 24

The Mountain of Government

"Early morning, April 4. Shot rings out in the Memphis sky. Free at last, they took your life. They could not take your pride." These lyrics describe the historical event of the shooting of Martin Luther King composed by the band U2 in their song "Pride (In the Name of Love.)" Nominated in 1985 for the MTV Video Music Award, this song launched U2's rise to international stardom. To date, they have tied Stevie Wonder for the most Grammy Awards by any artist of contemporary music with a total of 22 awards out of a massive 47 nominations. "Pride" demonstrates that historical events can inspire great songs.

Psalm 107:2-3 (NIV)

2 Let the redeemed of the LORD tell their story—those he redeemed from the hand of the foe, 3 those he gathered

from the lands, from east and west, from north and south."

Song Idea

Psalm 107 is in a classification of Israel's historical songs. Songs about history help us remember and learn from our past. Imagine that your local historical society called. They are looking for songs based around a local or regional historical event. Your assignment this week is to capture a historical event in song. In the space below, brainstorm historical events in your region that you might write about. You may need to do a little research.

Song Hook

Craft your song hook commemorating a historical event in the space below.

Songwriting Tip

Different song forms compliment various styles of writing. Story songs fit a AAA or verse only song form really well. Great writers know how to best utilize various song forms.

Title:

Music and Lyrics by:

117

Title:

Music and Lyrics by:

Week 25

The Mountain of Arts & Entertainment

Here you ever heard of Weird Al Yankovic? Though most of us are not familiar with him, Al has earned four Grammy Awards and eleven nominations, four gold records, and six platinum records. His awards and career span three decades. Al's success has come from creating parodies of pop culture by turning famous songs and music videos into works of comedy. His first Grammy in 1985 morphed Michael Jackson's "Beat It" into "Eat It." More recently, *Mandatory Fun* (2014) shot to the number one position during it's debut week and took the 2015 Grammy for best comedy album. But musical parody is not just for "weird" people. Parody for humorous effect was a common practice of composers from Bach to Sondheim and performers like Spike Jones. Al's career shows that there are many ways to influence culture and music as well as demonstrates to us the power of a great rewrite.

Psalm 126:2 (NIV)

2 Our mouths were filled with laughter, our tongues with songs of joy.

Song Idea

For your assignment this week, let's imagine that Comedy Central is releasing an album of parodies of famous songs. Look over today's Billboard or iTunes top ten charts and choose a song to parody. Write below three top songs and a parody idea for each of your selections.

Song Hook

Choose your best parody idea and write the song hook in the space below.

Songwriting Tip

Parodies aren't just funny or silly; good parodies usually contain a clever commentary on culture or society that is often subtly veiled within the humor. This is the genius of it's song craft. (Parodies generally fall under "fair use" copyright laws.)

Title:

Music and Lyrics by:

Title:

Music and Lyrics by:

Week 26

The Mountain of Media

In 2005, the band Lifehouse released a single "You and Me" that became the fifth longest-charted song in history staying on Billboard's Hot 100 for 62 weeks. Part of the song's longevity and sustained popularity is due to its placement as a backdrop for TV episodes of *Smallville, Cold Case, Boston Legal, Gavin & Stacey, Everwood, Grey's Anatomy, The 4400,* and *Medium.* The band got its start doing Christian gigs and church worship services but found that their songs could have a greater impact by writing for media and a mainstream audience. Consequently, songs like "Everything" have appeared in radio hit lists and TV episodes as well as still finding their way into church worship services.

2 Thessalonians 3:1 (AMPC)

1 Furthermore, brethren, do pray for us, that the Word of the

Lord may speed on (spread rapidly and run its course) and be glorified and triumph, even as [it has done] with you,

Song Idea

Practice composing songs that could be as comfortable in a TV placement as in a church service. Your assignment this week is to compose a song for the mountain of media that could be placed in an evening teen drama on the subject of "choices." Capture your ideas in the space below.

Song Hook

Craft your song hook on choices in the space provided below.

Songwriting Tip

A great song possesses what is called a universal song theme that compels others to say, "That's my song." It gives language to thoughts and feelings that all of us have. Don't allow a song to grow so personal that it doesn't relate to a more universal experience.

Title:

Music and Lyrics by:

Title:

Music and Lyrics by:

Week 27

The Mountain of Education

"Pomp and Circumstance" or "The Graduation March" was first played at the graduation ceremony at Yale University in June of 1905. Originally part of a series of marches for orchestra composed by Sir Edward Elgar, it is played as the processional tune at countless high school and college graduation ceremonies across the country. *Rolling Stone's* list of the best graduation songs of the last 20 years includes Miley Cyrus' "The Climb," Nickleback's "Photograph," Nicki Minaj's "Moment 4 Life," and Matchbox 20's "How Far We've Come." People who commemorate special days with well-crafted songs will always have an influence on society.

Leviticus 23:24 (NIV)

24 "Say to the Israelites: 'On the first day of the seventh

month you are to have a day of Sabbath rest, a sacred assembly commemorated with trumpet blasts.'"

Song Idea

Your assignment this week is to compose a song that could be used to commemorate a graduation ceremony. In the space below capture some thoughts and word pictures that you associate with graduation.

Song Hook

Write your graduation-themed song hook in the space below.

Songwriting Tip

Word pictures, images, and ideas that stimulate the senses help us feel what the composer is feeling. Great songwriting is not about self-expression but rather communication.

Title:

Music and Lyrics by:

129

Title:

Music and Lyrics by:

Week 28

The Mountain of Business

Before the advent of household radios in the early 1920's, Major General George Owen Squier dreamed of piping wired music into businesses to affect the productivity of workers and mood of patrons. By 1934, he had trademarked the term "muzak" as a type of background music sold to restaurants and retailers to stimulate productivity. Seventy-five years later, Mood Media agreed to purchase Muzak Holdings for 345 million dollars. Why did it sell for so much? Almost one hundred years later, music has been proven to affect the purchasing of patrons and the productivity of workers. The Bible often speaks of music's influence over human moods and emotions.

1 Samuel 16:23 (NIV)

23 David would take up his lyre and play. Then relief would

come to Saul; he would feel better, and the evil spirit would depart from him.

Song Idea

Your assignment this week is to compose a song for the atmosphere of a specific business. Choose a restaurant or retailer in your area. What ideas, images, and sounds would contribute to the productivity of this business? Write some ideas below.

Song Hook

Now craft a hook that sums up your best idea in the space below.

Songwriting Tip

Strong songwriters should avoid being intentionally or unintentionally obscure in their songs. Get to the point of the lyric within the first two lines or sentences. The song hook forms a clear target for our song craft where we always know what we are writing about.

Title:

Music and Lyrics by:

133

Title:

Music and Lyrics by:

Week 29

The Mountain of Religion

Composing songs for corporate worship is one of the most prevalent ways to serve the mountain of religion as a songwriter. There are many types of worship songs. This week we will focus on crafting a declaration of intent. This type of song details what a person or group hopes to do towards God or His kingdom. Chris Tomlin's declaration of intent "I Lift My Hands" received a Grammy nomination for best song and best album in 2012. With twenty-two GMA Dove Awards and fifty-two nominations, two Billboard Music Awards, seven Grammy nominations, and a Grammy Award for best contemporary music album, Chris Tomlin is perhaps the most recognized and celebrated contemporary worship writer.

Psalm 63:4 (NIV)

4 I will praise you as long as I live, and in your name I will lift up my hands.

Song Idea

Your assignment this week is to compose a declaration of intent that could be used in a church worship service. Chris Tomlin wrote on the second half of this verse, but what about the first? Develop song ideas around the intention, "I will praise you as long as I live." Capture your ideas in the space below.

Song Hook

In a declaration of intent, the song hook should contain the intention, such as "I will praise you." Write your declared intention song hook in the space below.

Songwriting Tip

If the chorus contains the intention, then the verses should contain the reasons for or benefits of that intention. In this way, the song hook helps us know how and what to write in the verse sections.

Title:

Music and Lyrics by:

_____

_____

_____

_____

_____

_____

_____

_____

_____

_____

_____

_____

_____

_____

_____

_____

_____

_____

_____

_____

_____

_____

Title:

Music and Lyrics by:

Week 30

The Mountain of Family

Over six thousand people per day get married in the United States — that's 2.3 million each year. Marriage ceremonies are a musical market all of there own, but so is the celebration of marriage. "Anniversary" by rhythm and blues stars Tony! Toni! Tone'! earned the group Grammy Award nominations for best R&B song and best R&B performance by a duo with vocals in 1994. They describe their song as a romantic, elegant slow jam with lust strings, lavish vocal harmonies, moody violin, and lyrics about a mature, lasting love. Composing for weddings and anniversaries can be impacting and lucrative since couples are always looking for songs that can capture the essence of these special events.

Hebrews 13:4 (NIV)

Marriage should be honored by all

Song Idea

Your assignment this week is to create a song that could be used for an anniversary party, ceremony, or celebration. Brainstorm some song ideas in the space below.

Song Hook

Take your best idea and craft a song hook around it in the space provided.

Songwriting Tip

Avoid cliché lines about love and marriage unless you plan to do a play on words. Many times in songwriting, a phrase that could be cliché can be cleverly turned and crafted into a memorable message.

Title:

Music and Lyrics by:

Title:

Music and Lyrics by:

Week 31

The Mountain of Government

Tourism is in the top 10 industries in 28 of the 50 United States of America. Travel is a trillion dollar industry in the U.S., and one out of every 18 Americans is employed either directly or indirectly in a travel or tourism-related industry.

In 2012, Brand USA hired Grammy winner Rosanne Cash to write and sing "Land of Dreams" for a commercial used to promote tourism in America. Songs that promote the love for or virtues of a specific location can by crafted for the tourism industry to form a profitable niche in the music market.

Psalm 137:5-6 (NIV)

5 If I forget you, Jerusalem, may my right hand forget its skill.

6 May my tongue cling to the roof of my mouth if I do not

remember you, if I do not consider Jerusalem my highest joy.

Song Idea

This week's assignment is to choose a local, regional, or national tourist attraction near you and craft a song that could be used for a commercial promotion. Choose your location and write a few of this attraction's virtues in the space below.

Song Hook

Often the song hook of this type of promo will include the name of the location. Craft your hook in the space below.

Songwriting Tip

Remember the songwriting rule "show me; don't tell me." The goal of this assignment is to move listeners to feel like they are at the described location or that they certainly wish they were.

Title:

Music and Lyrics by:

Title:

Music and Lyrics by:

Week 32

The Mountain of Entertainment

Michael Bolton in known for his pop rock ballads, selling over 75 million records and winning multiple American Music and Grammy Awards. But did you know that during his musical career, Bolton did a major switch of musical genres? From the mid 1970s to the mid 1980s, Bolton was the front man for the heavy metal band Blackjack, opening for Ozzy Osbourne. Bolton had even auditioned for the lead vocalist position in Osbourne's former band Black Sabbath. The point is, sometimes experimenting with other musical genres can help you find your niche in the music world.

Isaiah 43:19 (NIV)

19 See, I am doing a new thing! Now it springs up; do you not perceive it? I am making a way in the wilderness and streams in the wasteland.

Song Idea

Is it possible that your success in music and songwriting is awaiting a new thing? This week's assignment is to test your writing skills outside of your normal musical genre. Choose a musical style that you don't normally write in and compose a song crafted as a pitch for a specific artist in that genre. In the space below, write the name of the artist you will write for, their musical style, and topics from three of their hit songs.

Song Hook

Craft a song hook in the space below that you think matches this artist's style.

Songwriting Tip

We have said that the goal of songwriting is not self-expression, but effective communication. Great songwriters are not only in touch with how they feel, they know how to give voice and expression to others through their songs.

Title:

Music and Lyrics by:

Title:

Music and Lyrics by:

Week 33

The Mountain of Media

Gary Portnoy was just 25 years old in 1982 when he wrote the theme song for the TV show "Cheers." Portnoy said, "I think I got $150 for the "Cheers" theme. But all these years later, Portnoy gets paid every time the song plays anywhere. That's how music for television normally works. You don't earn much money up front, but if the show becomes popular, your royalties can quickly add up. Portnoy's song not only plays on "Cheers" reruns but has been licensed for commercials selling cars, Dr. Pepper® soda, and even insurance. He won't reveal how much he has made off this one song, but he will say that it is enough to live and retire off of.

Proverbs 13:11 (NIV)

11 Dishonest money dwindles away, but whoever gathers money little by little makes it grow.

Song Idea

For your assignment this week, let's practice writing a theme song for a television show. Imagine that the PBS television show *Antiques Roadshow* is looking for a new theme that includes lyrics and a singer. Listen online to the old theme and imagine how you would replace or update it. Capture some ideas in the space below.

Song Hook

What is your song hook idea for *Antiques Roadshow* theme?

Songwriting Tip

Pay attention to your song's conversational tone. Is it formal or casual? Is it classic or modern? Strong songwriters make it their goal to keep a consistent conversational tone throughout the entire lyric.

Title:

Music and Lyrics by:

_____

_____

_____

_____

_____

_____

_____

_____

_____

_____

_____

_____

_____

_____

_____

_____

_____

_____

_____

_____

_____

153

Title:

Music and Lyrics by:

Week 34

The Mountain of Education

The mountain of education not only refers to traditional schooling but also the multiple institutes and research facilities that universities partner with. These campuses blend the search for medical cures with scholarly research. One of these educational research foundations is the National Institute of Neurological Disorders. They report that 40 million Americans annually live with chronic sleep disorders.

A study reported in the *International Journal of Nursing Studies* discovered that certain types of music can help alleviate acute and chronic sleep disorders. This type of music for sleep therapy is often referred to as musical biofeedback or musical neurobiofeedback. According to the *Fiscal Times*, the sleep industry in America alone produces income of 32.4 billion dollars each year. Perhaps people falling asleep during your song would not be such a bad thing after all.

Proverbs 3:24 (NIV)

24 When you lie down, you will not be afraid; when you lie down, your sleep will be sweet.

Song Idea

The criteria for positive results in musical sleep studies came by choosing musical selections with a tempo between 60 and 80 beats per minute, a regular rhythm, low pitches, and tranquil melodies. Your assignment this week is to use the above criteria to craft a song that could be used to help alleviate sleep disorders. Write song ideas in the space below.

Song Hook

Using the word "sleep" in your song hook has the potential to draw greater attention to the problem of sleeplessness rather than focus attention on something peaceful and soothing. Write your song hook idea below.

Songwriting Tip

Great songs match mood of music to mood of lyric. The conversational tone in your lyric should match your musical sound.

Title:

Music and Lyrics by:

157

Title:

Music and Lyrics by:

Week 35

The Mountain of Business

Following last week's subject of music therapy, let's explore the subject of music for healing. *Alive Inside: A Story of Music and Memory* won the Audience Award at the 2014 Sundance Film Festival. The Hollywood Reporter called it "a gloriously inspirational film documenting music's healing power in Alzheimer patients." Though modern studies on the connection between music and healing are merely in their infancy, the concept is as ancient as the Bible itself. According to an authority on music in ancient cultures, you can read in many ancient texts, including the Bible, how a musical practitioner was called to treat various illnesses.

1 Samuel 16:23 (NIV)

23 David would take up his lyre and play. Then relief would come to Saul; he would feel better, and the evil spirit would leave him.

Song Idea

Rhythms, melodies, and vibrations of music can have a powerful affect on the human body. The music itself is a powerful tool that can serve as the carrier wave of the writer's intention. What is an area of healing that you would like to craft a song around, and what are your thoughts on how to musically target this area of sickness, pain, or disease?

Song Hook

In the space below, craft a song hook that speaks to your target without directly naming it.

Songwriting Tip

Make sure the rhythm and melody of your verse and chorus are not too similar. Contrast in melody, rhythm, and lyric while maintaining a single theme is the key to great songwriting.

Title:

Music and Lyrics by:

Music and Lyrics by:

Week 36

The Mountain of Religion

Mandisa Hundley's career began in the fifth season of *American Idol* where she finished in ninth place. Shortly after, she signed a deal with *Sparrow Records* and released her debut album *True Beauty* in 2007 which earned her the first of three Grammy nominations. Mandisa's song *"Overcomer"* took the 2014 Grammy Award in the contemporary Christian category. The song speaks to her own journey of losing over 100 pounds and her desire to inspire women everywhere to strive for a healthy lifestyle and to reach for their dreams.

1 John 5:4-5 (NIV)

4 This is the victory that has overcome the world, even our faith. 5 Who it it that overcomes the world? Only the one who believes that Jesus is the Son of God.

Song Idea

Your assignment this week is to follow Mandisa's example and compose an inspirational corporate declaration of identity. The song should speak to a specific characteristic of who we are in Christ Jesus. Capture some of your best song ideas on this topic in the space below.

Song Hook

Craft a song hook that reinforces a corporate identity. You might use the first person "we are..." or "you are..."

Songwriting Tip

Melodic emphasis is discovered by analyzing which word of your chorus or song hook has the highest or longest note. This emphasis in the melody line can drastically change the meaning of your song. Try altering your melodic emphasis several times by singing each word of your song hook as the highest note until you have found the strongest melody to enforce the message of your song.

Title:

Music and Lyrics by:

_____

_____

_____

_____

_____

_____

_____

_____

_____

_____

_____

_____

_____

_____

_____

_____

_____

_____

Copyright is Today's Date:

Title:

Music and Lyrics by:

Week 37

The Mountain of Family

Maroon 5 won their first Grammy Award for best new artist in 2005. Though their award-winning repertoire is full of amazingly crafted originals, they also released covers of several known artists from Fred Astaire's 1964 hit "The Way You Look Tonight" to Queen's 1980 chart topper "Crazy Little Thing Called Love." Creating a great remake of a classic tune is a great way to honor the historic craft of songwriting, timeless musical artists, and also draw attention to your own original material. Scripture reinforces the wise combination of old and new material.

Matthew 13:52 (NIV)

He said to them, "Therefore every teacher of the law who has become a disciple in the kingdom of heaven is like the owner of a house who brings out of his storeroom new treasures as well as old."

Song Idea

Your assignment this week is to create a new treasure from something old for the mountain of family. Ask your grandparents for their favorite song from their dating years and create a tasteful remake of it. If these family members are not available, then research the top songs from the year they were married and choose one famous title to remake. Consider making this an anniversary gift for your grandparents or a sound bed for a family tribute video. How will you update this classic? Write your ideas below.

Song Hook

It's usually not wise to change the song hook when rewriting a classic. You can, however, update the language in the other parts of the song section. Write the song hook from your remake below.

Songwriting Tip

You can spice up a classic song by changing the instrumentation, adjusting the key, carefully playing with and personalizing the melody, re-harmonizing the vocals, or combining classic and original song elements.

Title:

Music and Lyrics by:

169

Title:

Music and Lyrics by:

Week 38

The Mountain of Government

It's amazing how many songs have a transportation theme. Though it was never intended as a transportation song, in May of 1986, Bob Seager and the Silver Bullet Band released "Like a Rock." The song quickly climbed to number one on the US Billboard Mainstream Rock Tracks. However, the song's greatest exposure was in the 1990s through the early 2000s as it became the theme track for the Chevrolet® truck TV ads. The song became so popular that Chevy's "Like a Rock" campaign became one of the longest running ads in history.

Proverbs 24:3-4 (NIV)

3 By wisdom a house is built, and through understanding it is established; 4 through knowledge its rooms are filled with rare and beautiful treasures.

Song Idea

A great song can be used in multiple applications when composed with wisdom, understanding, and knowledge. Use those graces for your assignment this week. The Department of Transportation is looking for a theme song that can be used for an ad campaign to encourage ride sharing and carpooling. The lyric can speak directly or indirectly to the subject. Capture your song ideas in the space provided below.

Song Hook

Write down the song hook you will pitch for this transportation ad campaign.

Songwriting Tip

Melodic range refers to the distance between notes. When composing a memorable melody, great songwriters consider the strength or limitations of their audience's vocal range.

Title:

Music and Lyrics by:

Title:

Music and Lyrics by:

Week 39

The Mountain of Arts & Entertainment

At the time of this writing, Jay Z and Kanye West are tied for the most Grammy wins by a rap artist with 21 each. Kanye claimed to be a Christian after his 2004 release of the song "Jesus Walks" and again during a concert in 2014. Though still growing in his walk, Kanye has expressed a desire to work on repairing his image and bringing some more positive lyrics to his music. When a music star professes faith in Christ, many Christians expect the artist to change overnight. Our faith is a journey. We need to be willing to celebrate people's process and progress and be loving and patient with them.

1 Timothy 4:15 (NIV)

15 Be diligent in these matters; give yourself wholly to them, so that everyone may see your progress.

Song Idea

This week's challenge is primarily about lyrics. You are going to write a rap song that could be pitched to Kanye West for his goal in creating a new image. He is not looking for Christian lyrics but great gutsy rhymes with a positive life theme. Capture some ideas for your song pitch in the space below.

Song Hook

Write your song hook for this pitch in the space below.

Songwriting Tip

Great writers only include song parts or lyrics that add to the overall forward motion of their songs. We all know this, but sometimes we fall in love with a great line, catchy melody, or intriguing song section even though it doesn't really fit the flow of the song we are crafting. It is best to extract these sections and feature them in a different song more consistent with their value.

Title:

Music and Lyrics by:

_____

_____

_____

_____

_____

_____

_____

_____

_____

_____

_____

_____

_____

_____

_____

_____

_____

_____

_____

Copyright is Today's Date:

Title:

Music and Lyrics by:

Week 40

The Mountain of Media

You know you've crafted a great musical motif when just a few notes can conjure a feeling or image. Such are the first few notes of *Beethoven's Fifth* and John Williams' theme for the movie *Jaws*. Williams has won five Academy Awards, four Golden Globe Awards, and twenty-two Grammy Awards. With fifty Academy Award nominations, Williams is the second most-nominated individual after Walt Disney. John Williams composed the themes for *Star Wars*, *Superman*, *Raiders of the Lost Ark*, *E.T.*, *Schindler's List*, *Saving Private Ryan*, and a host of other well-known movies. He said of his success, "Any composer, painter, or sculptor will tell you that inspiration comes at the eighth hour of labor rather than as a bolt out of the blue."

Proverbs 14:23 (NIV)

23 All hard work brings a profit, but mere talk leads only to poverty.

Song Idea

This week's assignment is to create a background theme track for a sci-fi film battle. Try developing a memorable motif to start off your song. What instruments would you use to create this mood?

Song Hook

In this assignment, you don't have to use lyric. Still, your song will possess a dominant musical theme to establish your song hook.

Songwriting Tip

Melodic motif refers to a bit of melody, harmony, or rhythm that is a catchy phrase in your song. This phrase may be different from your main song hook and appear several times throughout the song in various forms. Proper use of a melodic motif helps make your song memorable.

Title:

Music and Lyrics by:

Title:

Music and Lyrics by:

Week 41

The Mountain of Education

So far in the mountain of education, we have concentrated primarily on secondary education. In this assignment, we want to take on the challenge of composing for higher education. The 22-time award-winning band Barenaked Ladies did this with their song about cosmological theory "The History of Everything." The song was made popular in its placement as the musical theme for the TV show *The Big Bang Theory*. Their commercial success shows us again the power of a great educational song. Thinking along the lines of the theory of relativity or quantum-field theory, choose any advanced education subject and compose a song around it.

Colossians 3:16 (NIV)

3 ... admonish and teaching one another with all wisdom through psalms, hymns, and songs from the Spirit...

Song Idea

As the Scripture tells us, songs have the power to teach and help us remember. Your assignment this week is to choose a subject of advanced education and write a song on it. Brainstorm song theme ideas in the space below.

Song Hook

Choose the advanced educational theme that you are most inspired to write about and craft a song hook on that theme in the space below.

Songwriting Tip

What do you do if your song sounds like someone else's song? First, ask the question, "How much of it is similar?" Your song should be at least 60 percent unique. If your song is too similar, consider changing tempo, time signature, or song form to reinvent a more original sound.

Title:

Music and Lyrics by:

Title:

Music and Lyrics by:

Week 42

The Mountain of Business

"The Eye of the Tiger" by American rock band Survivor won the 1982 Grammy Award for best rock performance by duo or group with vocal. In the first year of sales, the album was certified platinum signifying two million sales of vinyl copies. Decades later, the title song had sold an additional 4.1 million digital downloads. The song's popularity was greatly boosted by its use in Sylvester Stallone's workout scene in the movie *Rocky III*. The song also appears as number one in Fitness Magazine's top rock workout songs. The American Council on Exercise says, "Music is like a legal drug for athletes....It can reduce the perception of effort significantly and increase endurance by as much as 15 percent."

1 Corinthians 9:25 (NIV)

25 Everyone who competes in the games goes into strict

training. They do it to get a crown that will not last, but we do it to get a crown that will last forever.

Song Idea

Businesses pay for the music they play in the background. Many exercise gyms are moving away from radio music and commissioning original compositions for use in their workout centers. Imagine a major gym with national distribution has asked you to compose a workout theme for their business. What images come to mind for your composition?

Song Hook

Craft your song hook in the space provided below.

Songwriting Tip

The title of your song actually is important. People will search for your song by the perceived title which is often the same as your song hook. If you get overly clever with your title and make it drastically different than your song hook, it may be hard for people to search for your song.

Title:

Music and Lyrics by:

_____

_____

_____

_____

_____

_____

_____

_____

_____

_____

_____

_____

_____

_____

_____

_____

_____

_____

_____

Title:

Music and Lyrics by:

Week 43

The Mountain of Religion

Congratulations! You have hit another mile marker in your songwriting journey. As you enter the last quarter of your one-year commitment, you only have ten songs left to compose. As we've mentioned before, rewriting is a huge part of effective songwriting. Rewriting, however, is not limited to your own original compositions. A popular songwriting technique in worship circles is to combine public domain hymns with modern original song sections. Chris Tomlin, with thirty-two Dove Award nominations, used this technique on the song "Amazing Grace My Chains are Gone." Chris's song proves the power of a great rewrite.

Ecclesiastes 1:9-10 (NIV)

9 What has been will be again, what has been done will be done again; there is nothing new under the sun. 10 Is there

anything of which one can say, "Look! This is something new?" It was here already, long ago; it was here before our time.

Song Idea

Your assignment this week is to make something new out of an old treasured hymn. Visit a website like www.pdhymns.com and choose a public domain hymn to give a modern twist too. Write the portions of the song that you will keep for your composition in the space below.

Song Hook

Will you keep the original song hook or re-craft it? Capture your classic hymn song hook in the space provided below.

Songwriting Tip

Great songwriters expect to rewrite their songs several times. Don't confuse finishing a song with a finished song. Be open to revisions and input that will make your song stronger.

Title:

Music and Lyrics by:

_____

_____

_____

_____

_____

_____

_____

_____

_____

_____

_____

_____

_____

_____

_____

_____

_____

_____

_____

_____

Title:

Music and Lyrics by:

Week 44

The Mountain of Family

Stuart Mitchell is a composer whose symphonic work has placed him in the Classic FM Hall of Fame. Mitchell received massive media coverage in 2005 from Reuters, ITN, BBC, and CNN/Fox News when he deciphered the musical codes carved into the ceiling design of the 15th century Rosslyn Chapel and converted those notes into a symphony. Mitchell used a musical technique called data sonification which is the use of non-speech audio to convey information or perceptualize data. Data sonification has been used in many applications like composing DNA songs, protein music, and the sonification of seismic data from stars, planets, and volcanoes. Everything in the universe makes a sound, and data sonification helps us to perceptualize those sounds.

Psalm 69:30 (NIV)

30 I will praise God's name in song and glorify him with thanksgiving.

Song Idea

For this week's assignment, let's try a data sonification exercise. Take the letters of a family member's name and covert them into musical notes using the matrix below.

Use this musical note...	A	B	C	D	E	F	G
For this letter:	A	B	C	D	E	F	G
	H	I	J	K	L	M	N
	O	P	Q	R	S	T	U
	V	W	X	Y	Z		

Example: the name JOHN would be the notes C-A-A-G

Write out the letters of the name of a family member along with their musical note equivalent in the space below.

Song Hook

In the space below craft these notes into a song hook that is dedicated to the person you are singing about.

Songwriting Tip

Many great songwriters have crafted hit songs around the name and characteristics of a loved one. Write out the things you love about this person and consider using a list method to build your verse or chorus sections.

Title:

Music and Lyrics by:

Title:

Music and Lyrics by:

Week 45

The Mountain of Government

"White Christmas" is an Irving Berlin song reminiscing about an old-fashioned Christmas setting. Guinness World Records has listed the version sung by Bing Crosby as the best-selling single of all time. They estimate sales at over 100 million copies. National Public Radio voted it to the top one hundred most important musical works of the twentieth century, and the Library of Congress added it to the National Recording Registry as one of the 50 most important musical historical works. "White Christmas" is often used in government-sponsored celebrations because it captures the mood of the holidays without specific religious overtones.

Esther 2:18 (NIV)

18 And the king gave a great banquet, Esther's banquet, for all his nobles and officials. He proclaimed a holiday throughout the provinces and distributed gifts with royal liberty.

Song Idea

Your assignment this week is to compose a holiday song that could be sung at a city-sponsored holiday event. We never compromise the message of Jesus Christ, but we realize that like the story of Esther, we must sometimes adapt our method and message to what a king or government official can understand. In the space below, capture your ideas on ways that you can express the essence of a holiday in words and language everyone can relate to.

Song Hook

Compose your holiday song hook in the space below.

Songwriting Tip

Once you understand song craft, you can analyze your favorite songs to find out what makes them great. Use the knowledge of strong songwriting you have gained to determine the building blocks the writers used that most communicate to you. In this way, you can write songs that you like.

Title:

Music and Lyrics by:

Week 46

The Mountain of Arts & Entertainment

Hamilton is a modern musical about Alexander Hamilton inspired by the 2004 biography written by historian Ron Chernow. The music composed for the performance not only received the 2016 Grammy Award for best musical theater album but also earned the Pulitzer Prize for drama. A musical, however, is more than its music; it must have compelling characters who need or want something desperately, and that need comes up against an equally powerful obstacle. The resulting conflict forces the characters to risk everything. The resulting twists and turns of the plot are captured in songs with dramatic melodies and well-crafted lyrics.

Song of Songs 3:1-2 (NIV)

1 All night long on my bed I looked for the one my heart loves; I looked for him but did not find him. **2** I will get up now and go about the city, through its streets and squares; I will search for the one my heart loves. So I looked for him but did not find him.

Song Idea

Many historians classify the Song of Songs as a musical about romantic love with an allegorical reference to God's love for Israel and/or Christ's love for humanity. Regardless of how its applications are interpreted, we know that songs from a romantic musical were recorded in the Bible. Your assignment this week is to compose a romantic song that could be used in a musical. Your lyrics and music should express a specific dramatic need and how the character is responding to it. Write your basic ideas in the space provided below.

Song Hook

Craft a song hook that captures the main theme of your romantic musical composition.

Songwriting Tip

Most people find it difficult to refine while they create. Both refining and creating are necessary components to the larger creative process, yet great writers learn to capture creative ideas while they are freely flowing and save refining and rewriting for a later time.

Title:

Music and Lyrics by:

Week 47

The Mountain of Media

In 2011, Gotye uploaded to YouTube a clip of his landmark song "Somebody I Used to Know." The song launched his career to international prominence. To date, the song has 767,164,310 views! Two years after the YouTube launch, the song snatched the Grammy Award for record of the year. Social media sites like YouTube have launched many songs from obscurity into the main stream. After traditional radio, YouTube is considered the number one place people go to discover new music today. It is the public square of our day where people have equal opportunity to raise their voices and be heard.

Proverbs 1:20 (NIV)

20 Out in the open wisdom calls aloud, she raises her voice in the public square.

Song Idea

Your assignment this week is to create a song and accompanying music or lyric video for posting to YouTube. What kind of lyric or hook will cause your song to stand out from the rest of the crowd? Something humorous, romantic, edgy, or political? Write your ideas in the space below.

Song Hook

Write your best song hook idea in the space below.

Songwriting Tip

If you don't have access to cameras and editing equipment, you can still make a lyric video with simple free programs like iMovie® for Mac® computers or Windows Movie Maker®.

Title:

Music and Lyrics by:

215

Title:

Music and Lyrics by:

Week 48

The Mountain of Education

James Brown was called the "father of funk" and the "godfather of soul." Brown stands as one of the first inductees into the Rock and Roll Hall of Fame and earned Grammy's Lifetime Achievement Award. In 1966, Brown along with writer Burt Jones, attempted his first socially conscious song "Stay in School." The single reached number four on the rhythm and blues charts and also hit the pop charts. More importantly, the song led to Brown's meeting Vice President Hubert Humphrey who also had been working on a stay-in-school program.

Proverbs 12:1 (NIV)

1 Whoever loves discipline loves knowledge, but whoever hates correction is stupid.

Song Idea

You've probably already figured out this week's assignment—write a song that inspires students to stay in school. What are some of the motivations you could offer for someone staying in school? Capture these ideas in the space below.

Song Hook

Craft a song hook in the space below that you think will capture the attention of your target market.

Songwriting Tip

Song craft and structure is a faithful servant but a cruel master. Now that you have learned and mastered some tools of song craft, let them serve you rather than limit your creativity.

Title:

Music and Lyrics by:

Title:

Music and Lyrics by:

Week 49

The Mountain of Business

Most restaurants don't just plug in their iPods® and hit play; it's illegal for one thing. They actually go through a "sonic identity process." Finding a core sound for a restaurant is not about choosing one artist, genre, or era of music to play; it is combining these three to create a unique feel and special sound that matches the atmosphere and menu of each restaurant. When restaurants find the right background music, it can increase spending on average of $2 per person. If you only served 100 people each day, that would still amount to an increase in sales of $73,000 per year just by having the right background music. This connection between music and profits demonstrates the importance of distinct song choices.

Jeremiah 30:19 (NIV)

From them will come songs of thanksgiving and the sound of rejoicing. I will add to their numbers, and they will not be decreased; I will bring them honor, and they will not be disdained.

Song Idea

Choose an area restaurant to compose a sample song for. Listen to the music they are currently playing and analyze how it matches their menu and overall vibe. Now craft a song that you could pitch to the restaurant to promote sales. The emphasis of your song is not on food but rather mood. Capture some song ideas in the space below.

Song Hook

Craft your ideas into a single memorable song hook in the space below.

Songwriting Tip

The most popular forms of music in the average restaurant are easy listening, classical, pop, and jazz. Consider which musical flavor would be best for your target restaurant. Great song writers resist the urge to only write in the genres they are most comfortable with.

Title:

Music and Lyrics by:

Music and Lyrics by:

Week 50

Musical Metron

Musical metron is a biblical phrase inspired by the Greek language that refers to a particular sphere of influence. One of the goals of having you write with so many different targets over these past 50 weeks is to help you discover a potential sphere of musical influence. You find it by asking questions like:

- Which mountain or sphere of influence was consistently most easy to write for?
- Where did my greatest lyric and melodic creativity come forth?
- Which area did I most enjoy writing for?"

Answers to these questions can begin to point you toward your target audience which then becomes your musical metron or sphere of influence.

2 Corinthians 10:13 (NIV)

13 We, however, will not boast beyond proper limits, but will confine our boasting to the sphere of service God himself has assigned to us, a sphere that also includes you.

Song Idea

This week's assignment is to first answer the questions that might point to your musical metron or sphere of influence. Write a song this week aimed at the target audience of your sphere of influence. Begin your song ideas in the space below.

Song Hook

The goal of writing your song hooks out each week is that you would become a better songwriter by pointing every bit of lyric and melody toward one central idea. Write your song hook in the space below.

Songwriting Tip

Once you know your musical metron or sphere of influence, it is easier to find co-writing partners by recognizing those who share a similar passion for that mountain of influence.

Title:

Music and Lyrics by:

227

Title:

Music and Lyrics by:

Week 51

Song Rewriting Assignment

Now that you are discovering your musical metron and sphere of influence, choose your top three songs from this year's writing assignments that would fall within your metron. Write their titles in the space provided below.

1.

2.

3.

Proverbs 22:29 (NIV)

29 Do you see someone skilled in their work? They will serve before kings; they will not serve before officials of low rank.

Song Idea

Discovering your sphere of influence and focusing on those types of songs can help you become more skilled in your work. Your assignment this week is to choose one of your top three songs and practice rewriting it. Is every line as strong as it could be? Are there any filler lines? Are there any forced rhymes? Try to analyze your songs as if you were not the composer. What are your weakest lines in this song? Write them in the space below, then work on rewriting them to make your good song even greater.

Song Hook

Write your song hook in the space below to remind you that every line must point to the song hook.

Songwriting Tip

Often when finishing the rewrite of a song, I will find that I like the original version better. It's still worth testing other ideas to make sure your song is the strongest it can be before you pitch it or publish it somewhere.

Title:

Music and Lyrics by:

Title:

Music and Lyrics by:

Week 52

Rewriting Weak Songs

Congratulations! You are about to complete the one-year songwriting journal *A Song for Seven Mountains*. You've discovered the concept through this journal that great songs are not just written, they are rewritten. The Lord instructed the prophet Habakkuk to write down his revelations and make them plain so that other people could run with them. The refining and rewriting process is how we make our revelations plain so that other people can benefit from the songs we write.

Habakkuk 2:2 (NIV)

2 Then the Lord replied: "Write down the revelation and make it plain on tablets so that a runner may run with it."

Song Idea

For your final songwriting assignment of the year, choose your weakest song in the category of your primary sphere of influence and rewrite it. What's missing in this song? Why is it weak? Write your answers in the space below.

Song Hook

Would you use the same song hook or recraft it? Write your former or improved song hook below.

Songwriting Tip

People ask me a lot of questions about copyrighting their songs. This paragraph is extracted directly from the Library of Congress government copyright website:

> Under the present copyright law, which became effective January 1, 1978, a work is automatically protected by copyright when it is created. A work is created when it is "fixed" or embodied in a copy or phonorecord for the first time. Neither registration in the Copyright Office nor publication is required for copyright protection under the law.

Title:

Music and Lyrics by:

235

Title:

Music and Lyrics by:

Congratulations!
You have completed the one-year song writing journal *A Song for Seven Mountains*!

Stop and take time to meditate on your accomplishment. You can truly call yourself a songwriter. You have composed over fifty songs and explored writing for seven different mountains of influence. You have a better idea of what might be your primary target audience, also called your musical metron or sphere of influence.

Over the last fifty-two weeks, you have been inspired by the stories of award-winning writers and learned from a wealth of songwriting tips. One of the greatest things you have developed is a regular habit of writing songs.

Consider continuing your habit of writing a song each week. You can repeat the assignments in this journal, create your own year of songwriting assignments, or try one of my other songwriting journals available from Amazon.com.

In the pages that follow, I've included a brief section of bonus material on some ideas for what you can do with a finished song. Congratulations again on your amazing accomplishment, and may God continue to grace you to serve your musical metron with great songwriting.

Dano

Dan McCollam – author

Bonus Material
What do I do with a "finished" song?

1. Make sure every word of your song is saying something. Don't allow any fluff or filler words. Treat every word as a valuable space to feature your best work.

2. Submit your song to the critique of songwriting peers. If you don't have this locally, check for songwriting forums online. Be open to rewrites from suggestions you receive. Your openness and teachability is really important to strengthening this relationship and getting truly helpful feedback in the future. Once your song and rewrites have withstood some critique, you are ready to submit your song to a few publishing options.

3. Make a YouTube lyric or performance video of the song and post a link on websites and social media.

4. Consider entering your song in a contest. Song contests are easy to find with an internet web search.

5. If an artist asks to record your song, I recommend that you let him or her. The more publicity the song gets the better.

6. When using a studio or producer for the first time to record a song, it is best to contract for a single song.

That way you can evaluate your creative chemistry before committing to the time and expense of a full project.

7. If someone offers you an artist agreement or contract for your songs, spend the time and money to have a lawyer look at the contract to make sure it is a favorable agreement.

8. Consider submitting your song to an artist representation service like taxi.com®.

The Worship Writer's Guide
By Dan McCollam

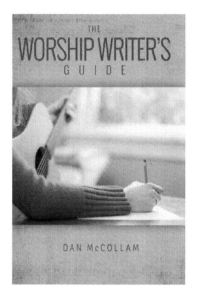

The Worship Writer's Guide gives you fourteen transformational tools for writing great praise and worship songs. The powerful lyrical and melodic techniques contained in this book will help you tap into the wisdom that will strengthen the quality of your songwriting regardless of the style or genre.

Finding Your Song
By Dan McCollam

Finding Your Song explores seven sources of inspiration for writing great praise and worship songs. Whether you are a first-timer or trying to bust through a creative block, the practical exercises and creative starters in this book will enlarge your journey as a worship writer.

52 Weeks Worship Writer's Journal
By Dan McCollam

Let Holy Spirit guide you through weekly inspirations, Scripture readings, song starts, and songwriting tips on a 52-week journey of inspirational worship writing. Compose songs of petition, invocation, and adoration, as well as declarations of truth, intent, and identity all while growing your relationship with God and His Word.

Worship Writer's Songwriting Course
a 12-lesson course in MP3 format
By Dan McCollam

Worship Writers Songwriting Course is a 12-part MP3 audio teaching in a live radio show format that equips you to write great praise and worship songs.

Also included are all of the teaching notes and 30 songwriting assignments in PDF format for an interactive songwriting experience.

You can find resources
by Dan McCollam at
http://store.imissionchurch.com/
or
https://shop.ibethel.org/
or
Amazon.com

Other books by Dan McCollam

Basic Training for Prophetic Activation

Prophetic Company

My Super Powers
a children's series on gifts of the Holy Spirit

Made in the USA
Lexington, KY
28 September 2018